in the *margins*

a book of poems

in the
margins

GARY K. OLSON

IN THE MARGINS

Copyright © 2016 Gary K. Olson. All rights reserved.

Publisher: Huff Publishing Associates, LLC, www.huffpublishing.com, Minneapolis

Book and cover design: Hillspring Books, Inc.

ISBN 978-0-9908073-6-0

Copies of the book may be purchased at www.huffpublishing.com/shop-books.

Manufactured in the U.S.A.

to
*Jean, my encourager
and love*

Acknowledgments

I am indebted to Jean Olson for encouraging me to continue writing, for her candid opinions, and most of all for her love. I thank Scott Tunseth for his valuable constructive criticism and for his skill as an editor. He has provided much helpful guidance as well as friendship. Bill Huff has done a masterful job managing this project as well as coordinating a wonderful team that has made this book possible. Most of all, I thank the many people known and unknown who, by simply being themselves, have provided insights, meaning, and delight to my life and to these poems.

Contents

Introduction ~ *xi*

a dream ~ *xii*

In the margins... *of experience*

in the seams ~ *3*
old cops ~ *4*
i like ~ *5*
grand-daughter at five ~ *6*
sixty-four ~ *7*
strung along ~ *8*
a too early winter ~ *9*
going south ~ *10*
march spring ~ *11*
a slow walk near white ash lake ~ *12*
air force academy chapel ~ *13*
distractions ~ *14*
brownout *(at the Institute of Arts)* ~ *16*
at the mall ~ *18*
leadership ~ *19*
complicit ~ *20*
simple pleasure ~ *21*
band of life ~ *22*
i saw two angels ~ *24*

the anniversary ~ 25
old picture ~ 26
a thin place ~ 28

In the margins ... of awareness

something calls ~ 33
to an introvert ~ 34
writing ~ 35
oaks ~ 36
university ~ 37
winter's promise ~ 38
spring leaves ~ 39
peanut butter ~ 40
awards ceremony ~ 41
good sport? ~ 42
inflation ~ 43
exclamation ~ 44
the 25th reunion *(thanks to Ray Anderson)* ~ 45
cleaning out ~ 46
grounded ~ 48
mulch ~ 49
cloud ~ 50

In the margins ... of relationship

taken seriously ~ 53
lost ~ 54
to mom ~ 56
arrhythmic ~ 59
dad's ashes 1 ~ 62

dad's ashes 2 ~ 64
sometimes i see his eyes ~ 66
hay creek ~ 68
old guys in a boat ~ 70
mother and daughter ~ 71
tying the knot ~ 72
with trembling hands ~ 73
grandson ~ 74
maple leaves ~ 75
we cut . . . ~ 76
he lost . . . ~ 77
type "a" personality ~ 78
it lingers ~ 80
getting the words right *(a hospital visit)* ~ 81
fishing ~ 82
neal ~ 84
admissions ~ 86
in memoriam ~ 88
barrier ~ 90

In the margins . . . *of understanding*

gratitude ~ 93
tracking ~ 94
life is ~ 96
thatch ~ 97
guilt is ~ 98
maybe foolishness ~ 99
applause ~ 100
a humble reminder ~ 102
integrity ~ 103
spaces ~ 104

liminal experience ~ *106*
in the library ~ *107*
camping ~ *108*
the season ends ~ *109*
are we ... ~ *110*
what if? ~ *111*
when things were looking up ~ *112*
mary ~ *113*
lacunae ~ *114*
the news *(upon hearing of a son's drowning)* ~ *116*
anecdotal ~ *117*
so ... ~ *120*

In the margins ... *of hope*

love's labor ~ *123*
a parable *(a teaching moment with Gerhard Frost)* ~ *124*
soldier's apocalypse Lynn Henry Davis, Navy & Army ~ *125*
beyond the bend ~ *126*
last moment ~ *128*
teacher ~ *129*
love wakes ~ *130*
attraction Luke 2:15 ~ *133*
funeral ~ *134*
light John 1:5 ~ *136*
easter ~ *137*
ru'ach ~ *138*
nerstrand woods ~ *139*
dawn ~ *140*

Introduction

The title and theme for my book, *In The Margins*, is drawn from my experience with public speaking. After preparing a speech, I review it several times. Looking for ways to improve it, I write notes in the margins: a possible story or illustration to use, a personal anecdote, a better way of saying something. Quite often I have discovered my best speech is in the margins.

Important things take place in the seams and margins of life. A child dances in the aisle at a performance of the Nutcracker Suite; a little girl, coat and arms open wide, trots through a flock of geese trying to make friends; a colorful butterfly floats and lands on mortarboards and black gowns at an outdoor commencement, a kind of blessing. In the midst of life's main events, things happen incidentally, adding delight and meaning.

I write feelings, images, and observations of life—mostly life in the margins.

a dream

I brought some poems
for you to read,
the fruit of whom
you made me.
There aren't so many,
my start was late.
I hope you like
at least a few.
There are some others
in my notes
unfinished—like me.
Perhaps you'll give
me time . . .

In the margins . . .

of experience

in the seams

When fishing streams and rivers,
it's best to fish the seams.
You lay your line along
the edge of currents where
water flows but not
as fast; where fish can feed
without the need to swim
so hard. You cast your line
below the roiling rapids
where trout lie waiting in
the easing water to feed
upon what's carried from
above. You lay yourself
along the seam where joy
of life can catch you.

old cops

Ev'ry Wednesday they meet 'round eight,
a dozen or so—some early, some late—
hobbling in on sore knees and bowed legs
from too many years of walking a beat.

Their beefy arms and chests, once hard
from handling suspects and lifting weights,
are slack now, like their bellies, good for
shoveling eggs, ham, and cakes.

But when they pause to look my way
with that practiced stare which says
I *have* done or *may* do something
wrong which calls for their attention,

I sit quietly, hands in
lap, trying to avoid
suspicion.

i like

I like to shuffle to the kitchen mornings
alone—open the fridge, it's little light
a welcome to the day. The coffee container
seems a friend I pull to me.

I like to make the coffee at start of day;
aroma of grounds, like smelling salts, tickles
my senses awake. Clear water poured into
the percolator—fresh brew, blank page, new birth.

I like the corner of our couch, my cup
at hand. Nearby are Ted and Kay with Robert,
Dietrich, Soren, Emily—my friends.
But first my thoughts, my inner voice, my quiet.

And when I hear you stir, I'm glad/sad;
glad to see you, love, yet wishing more
time I like.

grand-daughter at five

"I don't have any flavor
in my mouth"

What flavor would you like?

"Food!"

sixty-four

When you've been here a while—
hair worn thin, what's left gray,
your face etched—
people say things like
"You look good in a cap."

strung along

Promises are
untamed horses
without saddles—
beautiful—
'til you try to ride.

a too early winter

Only partially awake and bothered
by the visions of a restless night, I
pull the drapes and see what can't be so!
Corn flakes covered with sugar, corners poking
through the white. Survivors floating, I wonder,
or victims sinking with the vessel of fall?
Like my heart. *Too soon!* I say out loud.
I have gold to see, maroon and rust;
walks to take in the autumn sun, the soft of
green to feel beneath my feet—too soon!
In answer, dozens of maple flakes brush
the air and coat with gold the sugar white.
I am only partially consoled.

going south

Canadians are gathering as squadrons in the park,
huddling, honking their weather report,
giving flight instructions to this year's hatch.

Above me others practice a vee formation,
teaching cadets to stick together on the flight,
for safety, on the way to a warm winter home.

I saw you huddled with your cronies after church—
sipping coffee, staring out the window,
honking about what's coming.

    I know what's coming.

Your fingers fluttered like feathers 'round your cup
wanting to make a vee with snowbird friends.

    I'll miss you both.

Of course I'll long to see you Easter next,
but leaving spoils a perfectly good Fall.

march spring

The infants being born around us are dressed
in shades of spring's fragile innocence.

A few near the lake are draped like unfinished
gowns around embarrassed bridesmaids' bodies;

while other, perky, buds are pushing firmly
through early spring's sweater like excited

brides-to-be. This fecundity
stirs my desire, my anticipation.

Slow down, I think, *summer will come soon
enough. Enjoy this. Nature's foreplay may*

*be best, before its fullness in June makes the
thrill of new life seem usual.*

a slow walk near white ash lake

Yarrow, Beggarticks, Black-eyed Susan.
Sneezeweed, Fleabane, Red Stem Aster.
Smooth Aster, Canada Goldenrod.

Sun and Forest play a game like
hide and seek—Sun's "It" first—then
Shadow, hiding among the trees.

Bees buzz, collecting pollen.
Startled by a crack of twigs, a
rustle of weeds—a tan rump with

white bulls-eye bounds up the
hill—I got too close, still didn't see.
Am I in shadow or in light?

Standing. Looking. Hearing. It's so
quiet in the woods. Creature
eyes must be watching—must be

waiting to see what I will be,
shade or light, a mix of each.
I'll sit down 'til they believe

that I belong—'til I believe.

air force academy chapel

The sanctuary was immaculate,
everything in place, military style.
But of the seven altar candles standing
at attention, one tilted left.
The imperfection made me smile.

distractions

The coffee shop was early, needed
for Wi-Fi use to see the news.

A bagel and some joe would get
my juices flowing, clear my head.

But no. My eyes they flit from gal
to guy to old man's straw fedora.

So pack my screen and home I go
to focus in my basement room.

While sitting there, I saw the mess
of books and stood to rearrange them

then wondered if that Larsson book
were yet in paperback. And so

my car, it took me to the handy
bookstore where I was disappointed.

Now back, time short, I face the fact
that I'm afraid of meeting me.

Afraid that in the quiet space
there's something waking that will take

me where I do not want, but need
to go.   Coffee and Wi-Fi are easier.

brownout

(at the Institute of Art)

Lights dimmed and flickered, dimmed and flickered.
A docent touched my arm and
led me to the hall, an image of
Eliezer of Damascus
still in mind. Suddenly a
stream of school kids engulfed me
moving to the stairs like a wave.

Down, down we flowed away from
inspiration, the youngsters
sober and silent as though speech might
wake some ghostly specter.

Left behind in eery darkness, the
masters of light and shadow,
mirrors of life, the lamplighters of
insight, joy and hope for
every time—held their places
waiting our return.

Doors were pushed aside and as from a
tomb we burst upon a
living canvas of spring-green, emerald and
blue, Sun's gold glitter
sprinkled throughout. Kids splashed
onto that canvas, moved to a
chattering intercourse by the Artist's
aphrodisiac.

Shepherds appeared, raising arms,
calling names of schools and
students. The lambs gathered as flocks by
trees, on benches, near walls—
save for a stray or two—while
maple buds extended their emerald
tongues, a glossolalia of blessing.

Renoir would have painted his impression
but he's stuck inside.
He left it to ordinary me, I guess.
So I pulled out this pencil and did
the best I could.

at the mall

(a child with mom)

I know you cannot hurt me when
I hold my mother's hand

You cannot touch nor scare me while
near her side I stand

In fear she'd make you shudder if
one threatening word you utter

Her hand upon my shoulder and
my head against her thigh

I dare to peek at you and whisper
one risky, "Hi"

leadership

There were four school bands: an eighth, a seventh, sixth
and fifth—with each its own conductor. Each grade
performed from their own place upon the hall's
large floor. The closing piece, a Souza march,
they played in unison—with three conductors
attention paying to the eighth grade one.

Were they out of sync! And more than just a little.

Just then, soft cymbals could be heard in steady
tempo from grade five:
Chh, Chh, One, Two,
Chh, Chh, One, Two,
Chh, Chh, Chh, Chh, they sounded.
The others soon were listening; to
his beat they played. We rose applauding for
them all. Mine was aimed at him.

Great people have risen in their own time to lead
their people to better climes. None more timely,
in his lesser feat, than that young boy
who kept the beat from his back row and saved
the show. I wonder where he's leading now.

complicit

he caught a glimpse
    (sideways as it were)
he heard something
    (in passing so it seemed)
pretending he hadn't
    (much easier for him)
he never spoke
    (feigned his innocence)
he wonders now
    (their pain so obvious)
if speaking might have helped

simple pleasure

Flakes the size of nickels fell from
a breathless sky—many, so many,

as if a crowd above were paper-
punching holes in clouds—

gently easing down as though
caressing land with lace.

Parking my car in the nearest lot,
I watched them fall.

A child forgotten took hold of me.
Removing my cap, I stood and

let the whiteness, damp and soft,
moisten my head, my hair.

Lifting my face to the blessing, flakes
tickled my lashes. My boyish heart

said, *Do it!* So I stuck out my tongue
for a taste. What joy to be seven again!

band of life

In this Holocene Epoch
of the Neogene Period
in the Cenozoic Era,
Mike and Mazie sing along
with Barb on the clarinets
while Marge and Kevin join their altos
to Lee's crooning tenor sax.

The sound of Bob's silver horn
trumpets above the rest as Don
lays the bottom notes into
a firm foundation and Lou creates
some rhythm on the drums to get
the people's hands and feet a-tapping,
or getting off their chairs to dance.

Polkas or jazz, show tunes or ragtime,
the life in music ties us together.

At practice we kibitz and laugh, munch cookies,
have coffee, tea and conversation.
We're all retired from jobs, but won't
give up the harmonies in our hearts.
We smile and nod to one another
at the end of every gig.

Ages from now should someone find
this scrap in the sand, let it be clear:
This Holocene year we were
glad for the chance to play once more.

i saw two angels

I saw two angels—a blond, a brunette—between them nature's soft-gray beauty, ending life the way she began, diapered, eating pureed food. Those two, on either side, spoons in hand, coaxed nourishment in hoping for strength: "Would you like some peach sauce, Mom?" "The pea soup is good." "How about a little water, just for me?" Between swallows their warm lips nuzzled her cheeks.

Weeks before, those angels were shocked by the diagnosis, frustrated by ineffective treatment and unanswered prayer, harried with the pressure of arrangements to a hospital and a nursing home, humbled by uncontrolled body waste. They wept at the ending of a life that had nurtured them, a love that had nourished them.

But now, with an arm for support, a stroke of her hair, and "Would you like some peach sauce, Mom?" those daughters walked her down a road they did not want to travel.

the anniversary

of your death it rained
all day. A soaker. I jogged in its
gentleness at nine, thanking God
for drought relief. I thought of you. The night
before you drowned the long summer's drought
was broken. A rainstorm whipped the creek

to a frenzy, pouring into "Big Sea Waters."
Winds knocked down temperatures and roiled
waters into waves, enticing to bold-blooded
teens. I try to picture the joyful rush—
You never came out. Medic's carried you.
Your friends phoned us.

We've missed you. Of course we miss
what could have been—career, marriage, grandkids.
Could have been is fantasy. You
were real. I miss You—even your moods,
your outbursts of feeling, your impatience, your laugh—
all you were at eighteen. Thank you for that.

I'm rain-soaked now, eyes soaked
too, from pulling you back to life—and wishing.

old picture

Ted is dead.

I'm looking at
his picture, standing
next to me.
He's much taller.
We're robed in white—
the pastor and
his confirmand.

I liked him.

The untrue rumor
was he thought
himself a failure,
became depressed,
and when his wife
divorced him,
took his life—
How could they say it.

I liked him.

At thirteen,
we caused him pain.

*You're my worst
class,* he told us,
*the main reason
I'm leaving.*

His words bridge
the years between us.

Still, he planted
this seed, that
the calling he lived
might be mine
as well.
Think about it,
he said.   I did.

Ted is dead.
His image is standing
next to mine.

I'd like to see him
again. If what
he taught us is so,
I will.

Thank you, I'll say, and,
I'm sorry.

a thin place

When our son drowned
   I wondered where he was,
      if he's alright.
   Where is he? I thought.
      Who's caring for him
         reminding him . . .
I wondered. . . . I wondered
   like a father waiting for his son
      who's out too late.

This restlessness went on for weeks.

Then one night I dreamed
   and there he was,
sitting on a beige couch
   in a pleasant room
with a lamp on an end table
   casting a soft glow over the space.
He was leaning forward looking at me.

It was so good to see him!

"Hi, Jon," I said. "Are you okay?"
    (He nodded.)
"Where are you, Jon?"

He named a place—one word
    and I knew he was alright.
        The dream was over.

I was never anxious for him again;
    but ever since, I've tried
        to remember that name.

In the margins . . .

of awareness

something calls

Something calls my name at night,
wakes me from my sleep

Something brushes me when napping,
feathers cross my brow

I never see a thing, of course,
all in sight seems normal

In my youth it startled me
when walking through the woods

Never did it frighten me, just
wondered what it was

Middle years were frustrating
when wakened during the night

Lie and think and long to sleep
is what I did back then

Something calls my name at night,
brushes me when napping

Now I rise; I wait and listen
for what may speak within

to an introvert

You don't have to be perfect.
　　No one can.
Just follow the furry vole
　　of intuition
nosing to delight,
　　desire that wants
to move you to expression.
　　Risk some boldness
then, a daylight foray—
　　leave your burrow.
Boldness brings discov'ry,
　　confidence.
That last is tricky.

writing

At two a.m. my eyes popped open.
A prisoner was breaking out—
making its escape through
the tunnel of my pencil.

oaks

A row of aged oaks lines
the way we walk and others bike.
Arthritic arms reach crookedly
above, like a canopy
of watchful ancestors; a beauty
only the old can share.

university

'Tween Lakes named White Ash—Upper and Lower—ends
a road I walk whenever I'm there. A footpath
invites whoever treads its birch and aspen
hallway—entrance to a college of wild
but wholesome wisdoms. Profs of squirrel and deer,
of rabbit, chipmunk, feathers, and vegetation
too many to name, if even I could, hold forth
if you are still—on subjects vital to life
yet often ignored. And should you quietly,
so quiet, sit a while, Headmaster and Mistress
may rise to teach from the pond nearby. Branch
by stick by twig with mud they built a dam
and thus a home. The stream flows in to freshen
and feed but does not cloy. They left an outlet.
The water flows in to give them life; enough
flows out to feed the lakes and creatures about.
Would that all had PhDs like that.

winter's promise

The land is resting now.
Stubs of stalks stand stiffly
at attention row on row.

Retired but not dismissed
they are evidence of
fruit produced by plan.

A different plan surrounds them—
civilian life—
in ditches and borders, home
for field mice, rabbits, birds.

Tan grasses rise like winter
flowers through their snowy
cover, evidence of
seeming random produce—
fruit for creatures small.

Two plans, one promise of green to
come when resting's done,
hope for chilly hearts—
abundance for all.

spring leaves

are best born slowly.
Buds, little knobs, hard
in cool night temps,
peek at daytime forties,
fifties—wait, wait for
warmer stroke of sun;
then flesh begins to part—
a newborn green that stirs
the loins—then sixty, seventy,
lobes are spread in labial
fashion, as am I—a wonder,
making love.

peanut butter

If I'd saved the jars of peanut butter
youth to now, there'd be enough to build
a house. Organic jars would frame the kitchen;
crunchy suits a fam'ly room so well;
and extra nutty's just the thing to shape
the place I do my writing, while smooth
and creamy would be dreamy for the bedroom
I envision.

Of course the walls would be transparent and
the neighbors might look in, so of the labels
on the jars I'd make some shades and curtains.
This thought is all for naught, of course—I didn't
save the jars, but have this roll around
my middle from the contents I have eaten.

awards ceremony

No one should receive
this much recognition.
It tends to puff one up
and separate a man from
acquaintances and friends.

Then, after, at
reception, wineglass in hand,
he farted—loudly—still
one of us.

good sport?

No! . . . No! . . . No! . . . No! . . . I yelled
at what I thought a bad referee's
decision. It was uncharacteristic of me,
arising from some furnace deep within.
Surprised, I put my hand upon my mouth.
Too late. A game of basketball was all
it was. A sport, diversion, relaxation—
a respite from the rigors of daily life.
Not now. It just erupted without warning—
Sister's cancer, Mom and Dad's death,
declining income. Loss. So tired of all
the losing — no . . . No! . . . NO! . . . The hot
pot of lava bubbled and spewed, sending
ash onto the court of innocents.

A kind of therapy—released heat;
unless you're a referee.

inflation

Having bent to retrieve
two pennies from the floor,
I rose to give
the copper treasures to
a four-year-old
who turned away with—
"Those don't buy nothin'!"

exclamation

WHEN
i
SAW
YOU
STANDING
SPEAKING
BOLDLY
i
WISHED
i
WERE
NOT
AN
(i
n
t
r
o
v
e
r
t)

the 25th reunion

(thanks to Ray Anderson)

When a person who has not
seen you in ages says:
You haven't changed a bit,
it's not always a compliment.

cleaning out

We hauled the unused bed frame to the curb
for distribution. Doubles of lawn and garden
tools, gas cans, dusty cords, and hand tools
go to second hand stores. Half my
spools of string, twine, and wire as well as
old nuts, bolts, screws, and other stuff
I've saved 'cause, you never know . . . they go.
My faithful Mercury Mariner
is staying along with my too many lures.
The rule seems to be, *unused it's out*.
But memory is use it seems to me.
It's why that barrel of rackets, bats, and balls
was difficult. I had to sit and sort
this through—kept two—the football sons then grandkids
tossed around with me, laughter and hugs
passing for tackles; and the bat we used
to hit fly balls until my hands were sore;
the one you swung and smashed a tennis ball
into my forehead—laughing 'til we cried.
Memory is use.
It's why I packed some personal stuff into
a plastic box: old athletic letters,
music and speech awards, school annuals,
two report cards—one I'm embarrassed by—

freshman beanie, ancient letters from grandma
and mom. Perhaps you'll have a smile or two.
My finished writing is on a shelf, my notebooks
next—intention, incompleteness, the iota
subscript of my life. Maybe you'll know me.
Memory is use.　　　　　　I turn away.
I'm almost naked now.

grounded

He grasps a rail
to keep from stumbling,
fingers a wall
to focus his step,
leans against
the counter to check
his tilt; and when,
at day's end,
he opens the door,
she smiles and lays
her head upon
his chest.

mulch

I used to rake the dropped harvest of fall
into piles on the lawn. Our boys
would jump on them, rolling, laughing, scattering
again. We'd rake once more, bag the harvest
and haul it to some compost place where,
by nature's magic, it became a kind
of fertilizing soil used to help
bring life to other green and growing wonders.
Now the boys are gone to men. Well, one.
The other's gone to where we cannot see.
No longer do I rake up piles; it's lost
appeal somehow. It's not that I've no joy
of heart. I do, though dimmed a bit. The spring
in my step is slower though, dragging a little.
So now I mulch.
The mower and I make our rounds across
the lawn. As tiny bits, the leaves sink
into grass, skipping the compost site
to help our lawn next spring, giving my body
a rest.
A rest. I think I'll have mine mulched. Simpler.
Takes less space.

cloud

One long, wispy cloud
in a periwinkle sky—
impressionism's scarf of orange
and shades of yellow sliding to
softest pink—punctuates
the close of day, promising
tomorrow.

In the margins...

of relationship

taken seriously

It was a crowded place,
which served to emphasize
her gesture and his response.

As one of the little ones
so often taken lightly,
he leaned for worth to mom.

The tables set so close
for greatest capacity
made overhearing easy.

A waitress, having taken
the mother's order, turned,
and with respectful tone asked,

"And what will you have, sir?"

When he had ordered and she
had left their table, there was
a following with eyes—

"She thinks I'm real!"

lost

A little girl, she was just four,
and us, two middle-aged strangers.

She stood with fingers in her mouth
outside the shopping mall. She stood

and looked and looked each way she could
at all the cars so still. Though it

was cold in late November, she had
her coat wide open. As we drove by,

our shopping done, we saw her tear
streaked cheeks. "Uh oh," we said and I

backed up so we could be beside her.
My wife got out and said to her,

"Where are your parents, dear?"
"They got lost," she said. She'd come outside

to find them. "What's your name, honey?"
"My name is Margaret." Her fear

was vivid in her trembling voice.
"Well, Margaret, we'll go inside

to find your mom and dad, okay?"
As Margaret was lifted up

she patted that loving lady on
her back and said,

"We'll be all right, won't we."

I've thought of Margaret so often
these many years, and have asked

and heard her hopeful statement, question,
in various ways all meaning the same—

"We will . . . won't we?"

to mom

South through Coates, then Hampton
the view expands as it always has
for me, rolling hills of farmland
ahead on either side of the highway.

Sweet loam at rest beneath a duvet
of white pierced by stubs of harvested
cornstalks spaced like a bad hair
transplant—opens me to memory.

The land is much the same, loved
by familiarity—home.
I've traveled this asphalt often but now
the road of recollection calls.

The roads that take me home once took
me away, north by Greyhound Bus
but long before by experience and fear.
Survival and a need for hope led me.

Leaving you was not my plan;
escape from alcoholic behavior,
bad marriages, and poverty
was, else I'd have sunk into darkness.

I hope you understood the need
of a seventeen-year-old. Too young
to take you along, I went alone.
No longer. My roots tug heart and body.

Once I said, "I wish I had made
more money so I could have helped you
more than I have." "If I hadn't
been poor," you answered, "I wouldn't know

Jesus the way I do." Your answer
shook me! It angered me—yet gave
me deep respect for your faith,
a deeper faith than mine!

Now we are old. You are very—
I am moderately.
You called me home and I am here.
I lift you from chair to wheelchair.

When there I help you eat; ask
aides to walk you, encourage you
to try; read the Bible; listen
and talk; look at photos from our past,

remember. We remember often
and much. You have called me home.
We are on the road, before us
the rolling hills. We know where it ends.

"We have a lot to talk about,"
you say.

arrhythmic

Sinemet for Parkinson's
Seroquel for psychic stress
Klonopin for restless legs
Prilosec for nausea
Miralax to flush your bowels.
Should all this be depressing—
Trazadone for that

> *What's the rhythm of this song*
> *Drummer, what's the beat*

Shuffle-ten-steps-with-help, a belt
around your middle. "Do the Hokey
Pokey" and they seat you in your
chair—but you aren't happy, you aren't
gliding to this music's beat

> *We are awkward with this rhythm*
> *Drummer, stumbling to the beat*

Eat a spoon of ground-up pork
You've lost weight I see. Drink some
protein through a straw—"No!" you
say. "I need to lie down."

> *Help us find the rhythm, Drummer*
> *Please lay down the beat*

Sometimes you seem confused, other
times I wonder, then a clear thought
comes, a fine elucidation
We are thankful then and talk
about the life we've had

> *Help us find the rhythm, Drummer*
> *Help us find the beat*

Leaning on your bed, I look you
in the eyes. You tear-up and
say, "You know you are my first and
only love from high school"—

It is my Father you are seeing!
It's his voice you think you hear!

> *Help us find the rhythm, Drummer*
> *Help us find the beat*

"Will you read to me?" you ask
then you interrupt, "Read that
part again."
"I will not leave you orphaned;
I am coming to you"

"I will not leave you orphaned;
I am coming to youuu"

> *Could this be the rhythm, Drummer*
> *Can this be the beat*

> *Shooo pa pa, shooo pa pa*
> *shooo pa pa, shoooo*

"I will not leave you orphaned;
I am coming to youuu"
> *Shooo pa pa, shooo pa pa*
> *shooo pa pa, shoooo*

"I will not leave you orphaned
> *Shooo pa pa, shoooo*

Resuming our places near
the door by the band—
we await the last dance.

dad's ashes 1

March 23, 2009

Your ashes came today by UPS.
You died December 18, 2008
at home in Keizer, Oregon, half
a continent away from me. Your third
and longest lasting wife had said: *To be fair,
I'm splitting Dad's ashes among you kids but keeping
the biggest share for me.*

So, now I'm looking at the unopened box
and wondering with a smirk you'd like: *Did I get
your head, a hand, a toe?* There's no way to know;
and that's the beauty of ashes, no fighting.
Then when I opened the box, there you were in
a velvet blue bag in a clear glass jar which said on
the lid: *Jolly Rogers Candy*—your favorite.

I laughed and laughed until I cried and cried.

I wondered again what life would be like if you
had stayed with your first love. Of course there are those
who think I'm lucky you left when you did long ago.

You were too wild, too daring to raise a child they've said. Perhaps. But you've been different these later years—more open and father-like. And so, I have wondered fruitlessly.

But here are the jar, the bag, the ashes of memory. It's all I have left of you.

dad's ashes 2

May 28, 2010

Today I buried the portion of Dad's ashes
received from his Oregon family.
There really was no better place to put them
than where I chose. His parents, I'm told, loved
him dearly as a child. But when his father
succumbed to multiple sclerosis and died,
he acted badly and continued so.

He caused his mother pain; his sister and
a brother too; a girl, a pregnant child
who bore his child. So he avoided the draft?
The military? The Second War? Some think.
It is an old story. New, when it
affects you. His trucking and his drinking
were ways he ran away.

I missed him as a child. My brother said,
He'll never come back. I knew it too.

Three wives, five children, and, some say, a few
we'll never know. Perhaps. We'll never know.
He ran and ran for most of life from past,
responsibility, from self, from grace.
And then, too old, too tired, he settled down.

I missed him as a child. Abandonment
is hard to understand. It is a dark room.

You cannot find the light. It's filled with longing,
uncertainty, and finally, anger.
I made my way—and actually loved him
towards the end. But half a continent
was close enough by then.

Today I dug a hole between two gravestones:
a grandma who took your place for me; a grandpa
who died when I was born. I poured your ashes
between them. Home. You end where you began.
If not already done, perhaps you can make
peace.   Can I?

sometimes i see his eyes

He only talked about it once
while sitting at the kitchen table
sipping whiskey late one night.
And I, so tied to my life and time,
was trying to decide between
college and the Navy. College
I couldn't afford; the Navy seemed
likely, though Vietnam was rumbling.

He told about his time in World War
Two. He was a Seabee, clearing
landing places, building airstrips
so Marines could take Okinawa
and Tinian; Tinian
from which Enola Gay flew
to drop destruction on Hiroshima.
We fought too, he said.

*Sometimes Japanese raiding
parties would sneak into camp
at night and slit Seabees' throats
in their tents. I heard some rustling
and went outside. A 'Jap' came at me
with a knife. I grabbed his arm.*

*We hit and wrestled; I got him on
the ground. It was him or me.
I got my hands around his neck.
I pushed my thumbs as hard as I could
to crush his windpipe. I could see
his eyes. But it was him or me.
At night sometimes I see his eyes.*

His calloused hands lay on the table.
I looked at mine, then at his whiskey
tender eyes. *At night sometimes
I see his eyes.*

That fall I entered college, my privilege
for which he fought, and took my chances
with the draft.

Sometimes I see his tender eyes.

hay creek

We circled upstream beside a cornfield and through
dry stalks of aster flowers, wild and tall.

The seeds and burrs from prairie grasses spiked
into our boots and waders, hitching a ride

until we picked and dropped them elsewhere, spreading
their progeny. Exactly what nature intended.

We stayed away from creekside so not to spook
our prey. You moved ahead a space, another,

until I could not see. For that's a rule
when fishing trout. We came to this together

but solitude and spacing are part of it—
then relaxation and quiet patience follow.

And so, my graceful wand in hand, I slipped
into the stream as softly as could be.

My line was laid upon the water, arc on
arc, without a catch. But, undismayed,

I looked about at hills of hardwood, clouds,
clear water gurgling gently—thankful for

the beauty. Something was missing, though, and I
meandered east and west, as flowed the stream.

Then, a tug! A lift of rod! A minor
skirmish and some reeling. It was a Brown,

the prize! Silky smooth with brown speckles,
a few red highlights, it lay soft in my hands.

Its eye, black and deep, looked into mine.
Waiting.

Was this what drew me to Hay Creek? Were peace
and nature reason enough? And solitude?

Releasing the trout, I looked and waded 'round
a bend, another. What's missing must be there.

But all I saw were banks of grass and cornstalks
in air. Pretending to fish, I moved faster

and then, through asters of purple and white, your head
of brown I spied. Looking away, I cast

my line, content that you were there.

old guys in a boat

Corpulent filled the bow's high seat
and Lean sat aft and port while hatless
Shock of Grey-Hair ran the boat
and smoked from starboard in the middle.

They had rods and reels, of course,
and came mid-morning everyday
that we were there, again mid-afternoon,
to back-troll for walleye.

Back and back they slowly moved
u-turned and backed again, criss-crossing
where they'd been before—a kind of
trinity which moved as one—

a contrast to our still method,
anchored fore and aft. They've done
this many times before, we said;
they live beside the river.

They did not joke; they did not laugh;
there was no conversation. They simply
cast and trolled and caught. They knew
what they were doing.

I hope when I am old I'll have
some friends like those.

mother and daughter

It may befuddle a man who has
no frame of reference   who wonders
what has happened to his fairly
happy family

A woman   though   who's self-aware
and having this experience
will be more finely tuned   alert
abashed by it all

Her face has been more flushed of late
her eyes more red than usual
She's been on edge and frustrated
with things that don't go right

The girl meanwhile is taciturn
The changes in her body   feelings
excite and scare her   Both
Her mom is now the adversary

The woman leans and whispers to me
Menopause and a thirteen year-old
daughter do not go together

tying the knot

He bends the tapered leader back
upon itself to make loop one
then turns it to him, under and over—
a second loop. He circles once more
to lay the line between them. With
cold fingers, he pulls the second through
the first and has it. He hopes it's small
enough the trout won't notice.

Unlike the one we tie—loop one,
loop two. We lay our hearts and lives
between, then tug and there we have it,
                a knot to notice, we hope, to last.

with trembling hand

With trembling hand he lifted water
from bowl to baby's head.

With crackling, quavering voice intoned
the ancient new birth song:

I baptize you in the name . . .

This plump, new babe, this frail, old man,
in covenant with the unseen.

I baptize you in the name . . .

A mystery at work, a power
veiled in fragile things—

in hands like feathers on brow of silk,
one great heart beneath.

I baptize you in the name . . .

To unknowing child and twig-like man
relentless love laid claim.

grandson

His mother called to say
he'd been sent home from school.
He'd made a "poor decision,"
reacted badly some way
she did not say.

That evening he saw me enter
his brother's concert. He waved
and smiled—the kind that wonders
Am I still loved?

I yearned to go to him.
My hug might let him know—
I've been there. We can talk.
You have my love.

Instead, he moved to me,
wrapped his arms around
my waist, head upon
my chest—rested—
silently.

maple leaves

There they cower
between the mower
and fertilizer spreader
in our garage,
dry-gold hanging
on to green,
hiding from winter's
long sleep
as I cower
between I.V.'s and
your hospital bed
longing for Spring.

we cut...

your tree's limb
and carried it away,
the one that seemed misplaced.
We picked up twigs and brushed
dry leaves away to see
your name. *You should be here,*
I said aloud. *You should
be here with us, Jon.*
*You should have children who
could play with cousins while you
hang out with your brother.*
You should be here with us.
A breath of breeze just then
arranged the leaves. I shivered
but not from cold; I saw
your golden hair, blue eyes
and smile—wishing in
response.

he lost...

                    to the smiling pietists;
got fooled by grins and glad-handing ways
Their hugs of welcome and farewell
made him think they were on his side,
that he could trust their goodwill visage.

They held a secret not shared with him
and used the words he spoke to make
decisions that worked against him, left
him out. The hurt he swallowed felt
like Hell.

type 'a' personality

What do you do . . . ?

> This matriarch who loved her family
> had a heart attack. In aftercare
> we gave her helps for recovery.

What do you do when you think . . . ?

> "The doctors think it is the stress of being
> in charge and doing too much which felled you.
> We think you should step back a bit, ask
> for help, let others take the lead. Sit back,
> enjoy, and let them do more work." She
> looked skeptical.

What do you do when you think wherever . . . ?

> The counselor was wise and came with this
> suggestion: "When fam'ly gathers at your place
> don't sit at the head of the table. Sit on the side
> or get a round one so people don't see you
> in charge."

This lovely, seemingly gentle lady with silver
hair, fixed us with eyes of blue and said:

*What do you do when you think wherever
you sit is the head of the table?*

What do you do?

it lingers

He kissed her picture every night for over
a year. The next year she was pregnant, but not
by him. He put her picture in a drawer.
In time he wed another. They had children
and moved occasionally. Each time he packed
that picture but never told his married love.
Then, finally, he tossed it.

He is happy with his lifetime love,
but framed memories linger.

getting the words right

(a hospital visit)

How are you today, George?
Not so good.

You're breathing better than yesterday.
Uh, huh.

What did they do to help you breathe?
They castrated me.

What!?

Silence

Did they remove your testicles?

What!?

You said they castrated you.
No, no, no!

They put a tube up my bladder!

Oh, they catherized you.
Ya.

fishing

He hadn't been for a long time.
I was determined to reel him in.
So, sitting in his farmhouse kitchen
I cast my line again and again.
A quiet, gentle bachelor,
his puppy eyes hid determination.

*It's so early. Sunday is
the only day that I can sleep
a little later.*

But you could take an afternoon nap.
And think of all the neighbors who
would love to see and talk with you.

*Oh, they could see me here as easy.
Besides, I don't have clothes good
enough for church.*

It's not a problem. Lots of people
wear jeans and everyday shirts.
It's not the clothes that matter.

My shirts have buttons missing though.

Okay—I'll take them home with me.
My wife will sew them on for you.

    He shrugged his shoulders, raised his arms
in weariness but spit out my hook.

neal

Everyday he rose early, in the dark, and
went to work as lineman on the Milwaukee Road.
Warm or cold, snow or sun, ill or well he
rose and went—never missed a day of work.

Saturdays we only knew what we saw—
mowing grass, doing repairs, shoveling snow
at his parents' home, his home too.
Sent uptown for groceries, he walked and carried.

Sunday mornings, early, he ushered at the church.
Permanent Usher some called him—he never missed.
He'd shake hands, stammer greetings, hand out programs

You'd think this was his home the way he works.

All agreed that he was slow, slow of mind.
Something went wrong at birth perhaps; we did not know.
Most avoided him, left him alone, even his neighbor.
Never complaining, he simply did what needed doing.

Slow of mind for certain, but not slow of heart.
Much of what he did was done for parents and for neighbors.
Slow of mind for sure, but quick to care and serve.
Early everyday he rose to do what's needed.

You'd think this was his home the way he works.

Doing was the way he tried to let us know his heart, 'cause words for him just would not flow. Once, impulsively, he hugged my wife and me.

You'd think we were his family.

admissions

We toured the campus on a hill
with cornfields down below,
then listened as a counselor
extolled its many virtues.

While looking at your comely face
your fingers intertwined,
my heart engaged and stilled my ears
so words fell soft about me.

I saw a child, a little tyke,
who held my hand while walking;
a boy for whom his mother read
the stories which inspired him.

The car you scratched and had to pay
came floating in my vision.
The wart you tore so many times
when sliding on your knee.

We shot baskets on the tar
and fly balls I hit many.
You bring us joy in many ways
by simply being you.

I thought of cornfields down below
but could not voice my cry:
*You are our seed, our very best,
and now they want you here.*

*It must be so that we let go,
but please, teach well, care more.*

in memoriam

With a pick and shovels
they loosened clay and rock,
pitching it aside,

making space,

opening a room for
memories of
a life-time, a life-time of lessons—
a room they would visit often—
a son and his two sons.

They dug and sweat and talked.
I watched it from a distance,
too far to distinguish much,
near enough to hear their
voices, see their silence.
"Dad, Grandpa" they said
occasionally and, leaning

on their shovels, laughed
or spoke quietly.
They were grieving loss,
honoring him with stories
    of joy and regret

of gratitude and pain
of guidance and love.

Next day those three, with others,
stood around the grave,
his box suspended above.
I prayed and read from the book
but the best liturgy
was spoken the day before.

barrier

That writing is an act of love
I've heard and do believe

Perhaps that's why the thought of you
has often brought erasures

My mind is stuck on hurts and woes
and cannot be creative

The clearest word that comes to mind
is "pray for persecutors"

That too can be a love of sorts—
it's all that I can muster

So take this poem for what it is
a prayer for you and me

In the margins…

of understanding

gratitude

is a bell in the heart;
its clapper, often bound,
loosed by a kindness, a word,
some gift undeserved,
swings and strikes a note
so rich so warm
it wets an eye, caresses
a petrified mind.

tracking

From silver maple to neighbor's cedars,
paw prints in the snow reveal
our squirrel's journey.

A slightly soiled, matted path on
carpet—a trail of our habitual
movement.

It's said that Global Positioning Systems
can locate us by satellite,
while computer pop-ups

show someone is tracking our trail
of visited websites—intent
on what?

It is unsettling, this parsing of
our lives by curious detectives
who interpret, how?

It is unsettling to be so known
by those I do not know.

There is a place they cannot go.
Inside my skin where feeling lives
they cannot know unless I share.

And in my mind I'm free to roam,
to travel here and there, to dream,
to think free thoughts that can't be hacked.

Someday the trail will be no more.
The footprints stopped, the track will end
and fade to shades of memory.

Then only one will know my whereabouts.
Well, two, if I'm aware.

life

is a series of Nows,
each Now a house of feeling,
thinking, doing; museums
of experience
we visit on occasion
to see what we have been,
to learn how we've become.
We look and smile or laugh
and sometimes cry a bit.
We use what's been to guess
what life might be tomorrow,
which, if it comes,
will be Now.

thatch

I raked the sleep from grass today—much as,
on waking, rubbed it from my eyes—that rain,
like tears, might trickle into roots asleep
in soil and soul; that they might better bathe,
with sun and air, in spring's magic touch.

Upon the rake I leaned then—imagining,
anticipating new life stirring; smiling
contentedly until some gremlin inside
made me wonder how much work it's going
to be. It calls for tending, don't you see.

Assistant to the Gift, the role I play.
The Gift, no doubt, would grow without my help—
the major work's been done 'fore I was here.
But tending gives me share in joys to come
and so I rubbed the sleep from grass today.

guilt

is a useless emotion
unless it pushes you
to forgiving love;
unless it moves you
to correct a wrong.
Otherwise
it marinates
in mind and heart
sopping up
self esteem,
draining energy.

maybe foolishness

He buys a lottery ticket weekly—
once a week, once a week,
once a week—almost as regular

as daily devotions. He's wishing luck,
perhaps God, will do for him
what family and friends would not.

He doubts that it will happen, knows
that faith misplaced is foolish—still, once
a week he's at the superette.

The clerk, she smiles. "My foolishness,"
says he. "Can't win unless you risk,"
says she. "Maybe you will some week."

Maybe upon an ember blows—
a hope—that what went cold for him
will flame to life.

applause

There is applause—
a happy clappy
appreciation

A modest tapping—
encouragement
to try again

An *at last* clapping—
glad it's finally
over gesture

The soft palms melody—
a family
I love you patter

Then there is
the sound of silence

Your heart stunned by
something done

so well
           you cannot
move

Hands still

Breath hanging

Then

ERUPTION!

a humble reminder

The radio voice posed the old, old question:
*If a tree falls in a forest and no one is there,
does it make a sound?*

Not to oversimplify debate
about apprehending reality, but,

what of the fox in the forest, the bear in the berries,
the squirrels chasing tails. Do they listen
when the trunk cracks?

When branches begin their earthward dive, do
wolf and deer hear wings winging upward,
orioles warbling, sparrows chipping?

And when, with a thud, tree and ground meet,
do chipmunks run chattering for cover?

The old oak falls.

Small heads, I think, lift and turn to the world's
Symphony—even without us.

integrity

is that union which gives you
self-respect.

Sometimes it cracks like a
cheap plastic toy

when you do some thing that
does not fit the you,

you profess to be and
say you believe.

I've been without more often
than I'd like to say.

You try to patch it with a
drop of tears,

self-recrimination and
glue of vows.

The scar remains.

spaces

are places
you go
just
to be

to breathe
and brood

to gawk
and listen

to smile
to tear

without
expla-
nation

to touch
the magic
that's you

the magic
that's other

the one
who drew
you from
the hat

liminal experience

You can cross from
here to there
and step back
again

Here may look the
same and so may
you, but it's
illusory

Behind your eyes
and in your chest
you've brought some
there, here

Your view has changed

It can be good
for you and others
if you accept the
journey

This will happen
again

in the library

This window frames a pond
and last year's cattails, flattened—
an open space amid
the buildings, home this spring
to egret, Canadian,
and mallard. Mama goose
is nestled on her eggs
while papa floats nearby
to warn intruders. He
ignores a bachelor mallard
gliding forth and back
between them, eyeing the nester
with curious wonder—as
my thoughts glide with wonder
across that space,

that open space where juices
of thought and feeling flow;
where feeling gives depth to thought
and thought gives words to feeling.
Where nesting hatches delight.

camping

Dawn is narrow
as that swath of
road between the
forest trees

Head lamp glowing
burning toward some
dark primeval
lethargy

With your hand you
shield your eyes from
its intense ex-
posure

Turn away you
naked should—yet
crouch and stumble
to it's call

Rising like some
tadpole from the
mud and muck, some
Adam expected

the season ends

The Frazier shed some tears of green (though just
a few) as from its stand and through the door
we pulled it to the snow—as though upset
by our decision to end the season's joy
while it still look'd so fit and trim.

Our sheep and shepherds, magi too, will be
the next to go along with Mary, Joseph
and the Baby wrapped and in a box
upon the shelf. The grace of gift and giving
put out of mind until next year?

Old patterns will resume: We'll vacuum weekly
where the tree did stand. The dusting cloth
will shine the fam'ly's place. But will our hearts
and minds be wiped clean too of inclinations
noble—the gift we're given to be shared?

are we

    divine intention's metaphor?
The Artist's sculpture set in motion; meaning
predetermined or discovered in action?
The road behind us is an undulation,
a trail of grandeur and flaw, grandeur and flaw.
Its exegesis indicates the same
ahead unless we're frozen before tomorrow.
What then, if that should be? Is matter destroyed
or does it take some form we do not know?
Will God undo what God has made or is it
moved to other regions to be reshaped?
And what of freedom, so highly touted in
these parts? Perhaps it's we who do the sculpting—
shaping, shaping until God's love rights us.

what if?

What if the truth does not set you free
but binds another way?

What if the bird who's early missed
the worm some others got later?

What if the promise is not kept
but given to another?

What if? What then? Well . . . you

can hope you're wrong; that repentance
will change the situation. But . . .

you'd better embrace the days you're given
or you will miss life's celebration.

when things were looking up

Remember when things were looking up?
The watercourse before you shone as dawn;
each turn was filled with possibility.
You drifted but tomorrow would be better.

A storm raged, though, and drowned a dearest love.
You miss him still—this many years loss lingers.
Then later, for lack of an initial, a treasure
was pirated while friends and fam'ly kept mum.

You row in numbness now not knowing whom
to trust, the watercourse a breaking surf
and yours a tiny skiff. What shone before
is now from westward set for your return.

You look again believing it's still there;
but now you wonder when some help will come.
You put your hands upon the oars and pull.
You think you feel it flutter in your chest.

It could be disillusionment or hope;
they sometimes feel the same; but one looks aft
the other fore. You put your hands upon
the oars once more and pull—westward.

Mary

Magdalene has more appeal
the disciple more than Mother
unproved prostitute more
than the Virgin. We imagine

her harlotry: *And was she Jesus'
lover? Were they married perhaps?
Does their DNA survive?*
Humans need titillations

Could she speak, would she be angry
point out lack of evidence
plead an end to our gossip?
Or, would she be hopeful that

speculation about her
untrue or true, will lead us to meet
one she loves who loved her first
and discover we are loved

beyond imagining—as she
tried to tell us all along

lacunae

Substance is missing,
moved by eons
of evolvement
or by human
digging.

Something fills in.
Air, color,
wonder fill the
Canyon called
Grand.

Water settles in
many—rainwater,
snowmelt, ground
water rising—
something fills
spaces.

Diff'rent spaces
fill with thoughts
swimming one
side to the other—
meeting, mating,
birthing ideas;

islands of thinking,
bridges extended.
We could meet there,
share our likeness,
touch our diff'rence.

the news

(upon hearing of a son's drowning)

The only thing that I could do: lie down—
my heart and head too heavy for my legs.
An open window beside the bed beckoned
a cool breeze—a cold which pierced my chest
and hollowed it. Linen and lace fluttered,
fluttered, fluttered—reaching toward me: *Here!*
I'm here! Hello. Farewell. I'm here. I'm going.
I'd like to stay. Oh, please, hello? . . . Goodbye . . .
I reached to grasp your fluttering hands, your arms
extended to me. I tried to pull you, keep you,
hold you here—my heart, my strength no match
for where you are.

anecdotal

Artist of sunrise and its setting,
Architect of stars' design,
Engineer of braided living,
Poet of earthly delights,
Dreamer of joys yet to be—
It is my faith you are.

Where the hell were you? I want
to say upon looking back.

*Where were you when drought, rain-storm,
and lake conspired to drown our eldest?*

*Where were you when the inheritance
intended by loving souls was
diverted by one pretense and another?*

Where were you? I whisper into the night.

Forgive my impertinence.
Perhaps my anecdotal complaint
is inappropriate given
the problems of creation.
It's just that, being yours, I long
for you, need you, so completely.

Are we not each anecdotal?
And when we gather to a swell,
a company of anecdotes,
are we only then worthy
of your intervention?

Architect of stars' design—
we cannot know the distant you,
the abstract you, except by inf'rence
of your majesty and beauty.

But is that you I notice?

Upon looking back, that's you
isn't it—peeking, smiling,
weeping among the words.

Words—

as bits of hay in a feeding trough,
as spit-laced mud healing blindness,
as sweaty flesh on bloodied wood.
It's you amidst that world's debris.

And what of this world, older now?
Was that your arm around my shoulders
as tears magnified my sight
into the grave—clarifying reality?

And when in pre-dawn light she puts
her arms around me, is that you?
Or my delusional yearning.

Your sunrise and its setting moves
our hearts to hope that you come close,
the deepest, confounding joy to know.

So . . .

what do we have?
Illness and death are all around,
wearingly persistent.

What does it mean for hopes
and dreams?

Yesterday fills dreams.
Tomorrow teases hope.
But today, delicious today,

this moment—you here reading
in your burgundy chair,
me with yellow pencil on paper,

this joy we have for certain.

In the margins...

of hope

love's labor

Not in the mood for
    niceties
after what she'd
    been through,
she labored and sweat,
    warmed by animals near.
Clutching her wondering
    husband's arm,
she pushed and breathed,
    pushed and breathed—
pushed Christmas
    life and hope
into a world
    too long gone
to straw.

a parable

(a teaching moment with Gerhard Frost)

His was a suicide
and, no matter his reason
or illness, not acceptable
in that place and era.
They dug his grave outside
the cemetery's fence.
But time and growth have overturned
a previous opinion.
The cemetery's fence
has been twice-moved—and now
his grave is in the
    center.

soldier's apocalypse

Lynn Henry Davis, Navy & Army

On Okinawa's beach and at Tinian,
Midst sniper fire and sound of manly clash,
He saw the rider of a Reddish Steed.
But, save by fallen comrades' implication,
Saw not the Pale Pony's solemn guest.

In yearning breasts of schoolgirl widows
And hollow eyes of oldmen children,
The Black Horse cantered in his vision.
There in Trieste a glimpse of his family future,
But not yet the Pale Pony's ghoulish green.

Now with heart so limp, congested, pushing
Blood feebly through a twig-like body,
His sunken, vacant eyes mirror it
Galloping inexorably toward him,
The Pale Green Pony and its hooded horseman.

He has seen what is common to all
And in his vision shares a hope, a prayer—
That when the lethal hooves close in
And from earth his clouded sight is gone,
He sees the White One, loving, ride to rescue.

beyond the bend

Those swaths of straw invite my eyes to follow
their serpentine trail through the undulating hills
to where they seem to merge and disappear
around the bend.

Some local wizard raked it and let it dry to
this old-gold richness—like the road
Dorothy walked upon in dreamland.

I leave the highway until the gravel crunches
beneath the right-side tires and stop—gawking.
It's a pretty scene, a farmland painting.
"Beyond the Bend" an artist might call it.

I see you at the bend as though you'll go
beyond, drop from view, at any moment.

What's there in Oz?
I have my thoughts and hopes.
You've taught me well to dream, to trust the wizard
and all that's good beyond the bend.

Just one thing more. I hope to join you there
someday. Not now. (I like this place before the cyclone.)

Of course I'm not entitled, that we know.
A grace beyond must give me kind allowance.

We'll laugh then.   Won't we?
We'll laugh then beyond the bend.

last moment

A hand upon her brow,
my lips spoke ancient blessing
and prayer for loving passage.
I felt her move beyond
our reach, looked down to see
surprise upon her face.
I wonder now what awe
she saw.

teacher

Occasionally, a splash of color drops
into your life: an oriole's orange winging
across your path; a bobolink's bubbling flight-song
cheering the day; van Gogh's painting in Arles
with sunny hue.

You.

Your joie d'vivre. Your flair for the drama of living
you could not help but share with us, as sun
cannot but shine.

In quest for quality and passion for people
you drew from us more than we thought we could give.

Your hand upon my heart one anxious time,
you said: *There's good inside wanting to come out.
Trust it.*

Now, midst all that is within—You.
Your winging orange and bubbling song splash
the courage of possibility.

Though you're gone.

love wakes

I could not
wake him
could not
pull him
from that
waiting
room
to which
he'd
gone

I squeezed
his hand
and called
his name
to no
avail

I waited
with him

Then
she came

She held
his hand
and leaning
in
said *Grandpa
it's Linda*

His eyes
popped open

He stared
and stared
looking
his love
into hers

She spoke
her love
for him
said
how much
he meant
to her

They told
me later
that when
she left

he closed
his eyes
and finished
his journey

attraction

Luke 2:15

He attracted the strangest people: ragged
herdsmen, foreign astrologers—of course,
we think, who wouldn't be drawn to a babe—but later:
homeless beggars and wealthy businessmen,
the lame and blind, a priest or two, a woman
of the streets, a politician (who came
at night), the mentally ill, a potential
anarchist, a teacher, the divorced,
gay, straight, pretenders tired of
pretending, children (who receive so well).
He attracted the strangest, disparate people.
Love must be the reason; love, his center;
love unlike another; love that burns
away pretense yet warms you to life—
that lasts and lasts and lasts . . . and lasts.
He attracts the strangest people.
Perhaps I'll see you there.

funeral

I did not recognize you stuffed in
your grey-green, metal tackle box.
It was more green once; didn't have
that rust around the hinges either.
We know this look, looking in the mirror.

Hand printed on the lid, "Walleye"
Johnson, a name unknown to me.
Of course, I thought, *the you I know is
the you I knew when we were kids.*

We've talked by phone but it's not the same.
As kids we hunted squirrels in
the hills and, taking aim with your rifle,
you lit a match on a fence post at
ten paces. You earned my "Wow!"

Respect as well, for you could fix
things: radios to cars—and friendships.
We talked and talked in the hills of our youth.
I've not forgotten your listening ear
when it was needed.

So long, Lew. Good fishin' to you.
Save a seat in the boat, will ya?

I'll be coming along when
this spell of health is over. (Though
I hope it lasts a long while.)

light

John 1:5

Candle
Fireplace
Lamp
and Lighthouse,
symbols of comforting, guiding light.

None so dear as that which burns, our
deepest longing–
"The light" which
"shines in the
darkness,"
which "the darkness did not overcome."

easter

in spring
my heart
rejoices—
a twitter-
ing
flittering
sparrow
eyeing
soaring
eagle—
someday
someday

ru'ach

As breath it moves
across the life,
refreshing in heat,
chilling in cold,
caressing leaves
to giggling chatter,
enticing snow
to skate the lake.
The window shade
a gentle bellows
invites a nose
from out its cover
in the Valley of Bones
to breathe afresh.

nerstrand woods

This gold, ferruginous fall awakes my sense
of much that is around: aroma of leaves
fallen, damp, a faintly pungent air—
as autumn's drying tobacco; the rasp of those
already dry beneath our feet; the husk-
clad gold of heavy ears sagging earthward,
being picked and shelled. The close of harvest
suddenly here—a season of slumber ahead.
We walk together as we have for years.
The forest trees, leafless, grant us view
of creek and valley, water falling—hidden
when trees were cloaked; a new view quiets us.
In dream I see us as we were, clothed
with youthful vigor; now your silver beauty
shines. You reach to straighten my collar; I think,
It seems unlikely, but fitting, if we could close
together.

dawn

a
welcome
painted
orange
with
Hope—

811
OLS
NO CKO's NEW ✓11/23

6/02/23